HR Approved Ways
To Tell Coworkers
They're STUPID

60 Witty Alternatives for Those Things
You Want to Say At Work But Can't

This book is for entertainment purposes only. No certified HR professional was involved in the creation of this humor book. Use it at your own discretion.

"I agree with you
but we would be
both wrong."

"Sharp as a marble, that one."

"Intelligent thoughts have always followed him, but he was faster."

"They only got two brain cells an both of them are fighting for third place."

"Couldn't pour water out of a boot with instructions on the heel."

"It's better to be silent and thought a fool than to speak and remove all doubt."

"When it was raining brains, you had an umbrella."

"A common mistake that people make when trying to design something completely foolproof is to underestimate the ingenuity of complete fools."

"You aren't the biggest idiot in the world but you better hope they don't die."

"You're the reason we have warning labels."

"If you were half as smart as you think you are, you'd be twice as smart as you really are."

"A village somewhere is missing their idiot."

"His train of thought is still boarding at the station."

"The wheel is spinning, but the hamster is dead."

"He needs to carry a plant to make up for the oxygen he's wasting."

"I can explain it again, if you'd like, but I can't understand for you."

"If your brains were dynamite there wouldn't be enough to blow your hat off."

"I not sure I fully grasp your perspective. Can you explain it further?"

"I'm having difficulty grasping the key points of your discussion. Could you please provide more context or clarification?"

"I've noticed a task that falls outside the the usual scope of my role. Could we discuss how best to handle this responsibility?"

"The work enviroment seems a bit chaos. Perhaps we can explore ways to enhance organizational efficiency and communication."

"The scope of my responsibilities seems to have expanded beyond my current compensation. Can we discuss a potential adjustment?"

"The current situation appears to be quite complex. Let's work together to untangle the details and find a solution."

"I've noticed some challenges in understanding certain aspects of the task. Can we schedule some time to go over the details and ensure alignment?"

"I may need more explicit guidance to fully understand expectations. Can we discuss and specific objectives to ensure alignment?"

"I sent an important email regarding [topic]. I'd appreciate it if you could take a moment to review it, as it contains crucial information for our upcoming tasks."

"I see where you're coming from, but I have a different perspective. Let's analyze the details together to ensure we reach the best solution."

"If stupidity were an art form, you'd be a Picasso."

"You're so bright, I need sunglasses just to listen to your ideas."

"You're like a riddle —complex and often puzzling."

"You're the curveball in our team's baseball game —unexpected and a bit hard to catch."

"Your reasoning often feels likes a labyrinth -intricate and full of dead ends."

"You're like a suspens movie – full of twists and turns and not always making sense."

"You're like a mystery wrapped in an enigma, wrapped in a poor decision."

"Your ideas are like a maze – people get lost trying to follow them."

"Your logic is like a choose-your-own-adventure book – full of unexpected detours."

"You're the human embodiment of a 'plot twist'."

"You're the office's magic 8-ball-your answers are always unpredictable."

"You're the human equivalent of a 'glitch in the matric'."

"Your work is like a patchwork quilt- a little bit of everything, but not always matching."

"You're like a walking cliffhanger—always leaving us guessing."

"You're the emoji of conversations-colorful but not always clear."

"You're like a magic 8-ball – your answers are always a bit too vague."

"Your project management style is like a Roomba-it goes everywhere but doesn't always clean up."

"Your execution is like a mirage – always promising but never quite materializing."

"You're a perfect example of what happens when intelligence takes a vacation."

"You must have been absent on the day they haned out common sense."

"Yeah keep rolling your eyes... maybe you'll find somthing useful black there."

"I'm not responsible for what my face doese when you talk."

"I'd love to stay and chitchat, but I'm allergic to idiots."

"This idea is a bit like an exotic plant —hard to maintain in this climate."

"The probability of this idea succeeding is... interesting. Let's crunch some more numbers."

"I'm stretching to understand your point. Let's flex our thinking muscles here."

"This idea seems like a mystery novel with missing pages. Let's piece it together."

"Your ideas is like an unstable compoud. Let's add some elements to stabilize it."

"That's a rare species of thought. Let's observe it in its natural habitat for a while."

"Your idea is like a distant star – hard to grasp but possibly brilliant."

"Your thought process defies the laws of logic. Einstein would be intrigued!"

"Digging deep for those ideas. I see. Let's brush off some of the dirt and see what we've got."

"That's an interesting take. What era of history are you referencing?

Printed in Great Britain
by Amazon